BALTIMORE
ORIOLES

by Ray Frager

Published by ABDO Publishing Company, 8000 West 78th Street, Edina, Minnesota 55439. Copyright © 2011 by Abdo Consulting Group, Inc. International copyrights reserved in all countries. No part of this book may be reproduced in any form without written permission from the publisher. SportsZone™ is a trademark and logo of ABDO Publishing Company.

Printed in the United States of America,
North Mankato, Minnesota
112010
012011

 THIS BOOK CONTAINS AT LEAST 10% RECYCLED MATERIALS.

Editor: Matt Tustison
Copy Editor: Nicholas Cafarelli
Interior Design and Production: Christa Schneider
Cover Design: Christa Schneider

Photo Credits: Gail Burton/AP Images, cover; Tom Olmscheid/AP Images, 1; Roberto Borea/AP Images, 4, 32, 43 (middle), 47; Denis Paquin/AP Images, 7; AP Images, 8, 11, 13, 14, 16, 20, 22, 25, 42 (top, middle, bottom), 43 (top); Bob Daugherty/AP Images, 19; Ron Frehm/AP Images, 26; Mark Duncan/AP Images, 28; Ted Mathias/AP Images, 31; Mark Lennihan/AP Images, 35, 43 (bottom); Nick Wass/AP Images, 36; Charles Krupa/AP Images, 39; Charles Rex Arbogast/AP Images, 41; Dave Hammond/AP Images, 44

Library of Congress Cataloging-in-Publication Data
Frager, Ray.
  Baltimore Orioles / by Ray Frager.
     p. cm. — (Inside MLB)
  Includes index.
  ISBN 978-1-61714-036-5
  1. Baltimore Orioles (Baseball team)—History—Juvenile literature. I. Title.
  GV875.B2F73 2011
  796.357'640975271—dc22
                        2010036557

TABLE OF CONTENTS

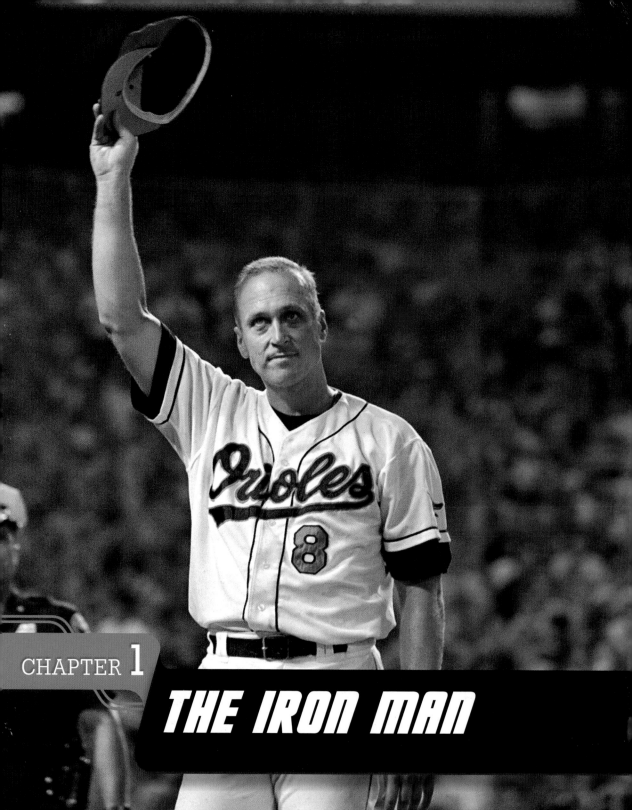

CHAPTER 1

THE IRON MAN

During the Baltimore Orioles' 1995 season, the most important number was a countdown. Fans followed this more than the team's win total or any player's number of home runs. And, actually, the countdown was a count-up.

There was a banner hung on the side of the B&O warehouse, way past the right-field wall at Oriole Park at Camden Yards. The banner was keeping track of how many games in a row the Orioles' All-Star shortstop, Cal Ripken Jr., had played.

During each home game, the number would change. Fans would have another reason to cheer. Ripken was on his way to breaking one of baseball's most "unbreakable" records—the 2,130 games in a row played by New York Yankees Hall of Famer Lou Gehrig.

Ripken did more than just show up for work every day. He won the American League (AL) Rookie of the Year Award in 1982. He was named the league's Most Valuable Player

Cal Ripken Jr. tips his hat to the crowd in Baltimore on September 6, 1995, after his record 2,131st consecutive game played became official.

(MVP) in 1983 and 1991. He even caught the last out when the Orioles won the World Series in 1983.

On the night of September 6, 1995, he played in his 2,131st straight game. This broke Gehrig's record. When the game became official in the middle of the fifth inning, the banner changed to the magic number. The fans cheered like never before. Ripken came out of the dugout to wave to them. But that would not be enough. Urged on by teammates, Ripken took a lap around the field at Camden Yards. He shook hands and exchanged high fives as he went.

One person watching in the stands was his father, Cal Ripken Sr. He had been a pro baseball player, coach, and manager. He had taught Cal Jr. how to play. Cal Sr. had been Cal Jr.'s coach and even his manager with the Orioles.

"The Streak" did not stop that night. Ripken ended up playing 2,632 games in a row before he finally sat out a game near the end of the 1998 season. By the time he retired after the 2001 season, Ripken had lots of other impressive numbers too. He set an AL record by making 19 All-Star teams. And he became just the seventh major league player ever to get at least 400 home runs along with at least 3,000 hits.

But, most importantly, Ripken is remembered as baseball's all-time "Iron Man." His 2,632 consecutive games just might be an unbreakable record.

Cal Ripken Jr. gets ready to speak to the crowd after the Orioles' 4–2 win over the Angels on September 6, 1995. Ripken had just broken Lou Gehrig's record for games played in a row.

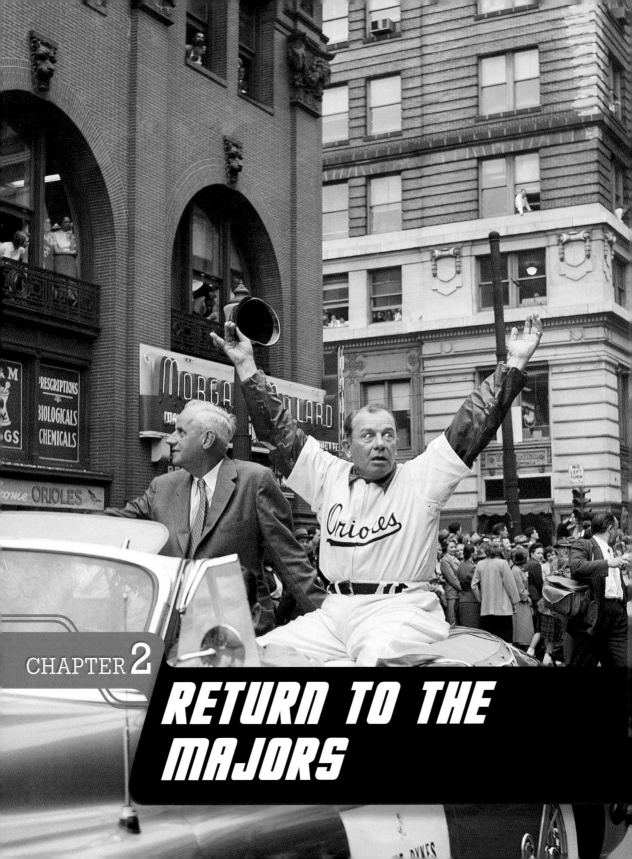

CHAPTER 2

RETURN TO THE MAJORS

Baltimore Orioles teams played in the National League (NL) in the 1890s and in the AL in the early 1900s. Baltimore also fielded a minor league Orioles team for 50 years. However, the city did not get another major league club until 1954. That year, the former St. Louis Browns began play as the Orioles.

The Browns' franchise began in 1894 as the Milwaukee Brewers of the Western League. The Western League became the AL, which in turn gained major league status in 1901. This was more than two decades after the NL had done so. The Brewers moved to St. Louis and became the Browns in 1902. The Browns were a perennially losing AL team. They very much played second fiddle to the powerful NL Cardinals in the hearts of St. Louis fans.

The Browns were mostly terrible in their 52 seasons in St. Louis. They did have some notable players, however.

Orioles manager Jimmy Dykes acknowledges spectators during a parade on April 15, 1954. Big-league baseball was back in Baltimore for the first time in 52 years.

THE EARLY ORIOLES

The first major league Orioles included great teams. In the 1890s, the Orioles played eight seasons in the NL. They won three straight league titles from 1894 to 1896. Their players included Hall of Famers John McGraw, Hughie Jennings, and Willie Keeler. Keeler was nicknamed "Wee Willie" because he was only 5-foot-4. But he was an outstanding hitter and became famous for describing his hitting style this way: "I hit 'em where they ain't."

The NL Orioles played their last season in 1899, after most of their best players had been sold to the Brooklyn team. In 1901 and 1902, there was a Baltimore Orioles team in the AL, but the club moved to New York in 1903. The team's first nickname in New York was the Highlanders. Then, in 1913, the Highlanders became the Yankees, who would in time be the most famous team in all of baseball.

One of them was Hall of Famer George Sisler. Sisler, a first baseman, batted .407 and set a major league record with 257 hits in 1920.

In 1944, the Browns finished 89–65. They won the AL crown and advanced to their only World Series. However, they lost four games to two to the Cardinals in an all-St. Louis World Series.

St. Louis, Missouri, proved to be too small of a city to have two thriving major league teams. After the 1953 season, owners of the other big-league teams approved the sale of the Browns to a Baltimore group and the transfer of the team to Maryland.

When the time came for the Orioles to play their first

Hall of Famer George Sisler was a star first baseman for the St. Louis Browns, who later became the Baltimore Orioles.

game in the renovated and newly named Memorial Stadium, fans could not contain their excitement. On April 15, 1954, about 350,000 people lined the streets of Baltimore for a parade that took the team to the ballpark for its first game.

The Orioles were still mostly made up of players who had been on the lackluster Browns teams, so they lost 100 games that year. But Baltimore was so happy to have big-league baseball that the Orioles drew more than 1 million fans.

In their second season, the Orioles put one man—Paul Richards—in charge of the team on and off the field. They named him manager and general manager.

Richards stayed with the Orioles until September 1961. Though they never won a pennant when he was there, he helped turn the club into a

Babe's Birthplace

Babe Ruth, considered by some as baseball's greatest player, was born and grew up in Baltimore. He briefly played for the minor league Orioles. Team owner Jack Dunn had seen Ruth, who was then mostly a pitcher, play for his school team. Dunn signed Ruth, then only 19, to a professional contract. The Boston Red Sox bought Ruth's contract during his one Orioles season. He became a star pitcher in Boston before moving on to the New York Yankees and emerging as baseball's greatest home-run hitter.

professional organization and brought in players who would be crucial to their later success. These players included Brooks Robinson, Steve Barber, and Boog Powell.

Even before Richards left, the Orioles showed that they could be contenders. In 1960, they won 89 games and finished second to the Yankees. The next year, Baltimore finished

Orioles general manager/manager Paul Richards, *right*, shakes hands with Yankees manager Casey Stengel before the teams played in 1958.

third, but it won 95 games. In 1961, first baseman Jim Gentile had a standout season. He hit 46 home runs and collected 141 runs batted in (RBIs).

From 1960 through 1965, the Orioles had only one losing season and won more than 90 games in three seasons.

Baltimore was showing signs of the strengths that the team would become known for: pitching and defense. Barber became the Orioles' first 20-game winner in 1963. At third base, Robinson began winning the Gold Glove as the best fielder at his position every year.

CHAPTER 3

BREAKTHROUGH

The 1966 season for the Orioles really began to take shape in December 1965. That was when Baltimore made one of the most important trades in baseball history. The Orioles acquired All-Star outfielder Frank Robinson from the Cincinnati Reds for pitcher Milt Pappas and two other players.

Robinson had a combination of power and speed that made him among baseball's best players. But the Reds decided that they wanted more pitching help. Cincinnati's general manager, Bill DeWitt, said although Robinson was only 30 years old—still in the prime years—he was "not a young 30."

Big Blast

Baltimore's Memorial Stadium had lots of room beyond the fences. Home runs did not leave the stadium. Until Frank Robinson came to the team, that is. On May 8, 1966, he became the only player to hit a fair ball out of Memorial Stadium. Robinson's home-run ball, against the Cleveland Indians, left the ballpark beyond the left-field bleachers.

Baltimore's Frank Robinson, *left*, and Brooks Robinson pose after the Orioles defeated the Dodgers 5–2 in Game 1 of the 1966 World Series.

Frank Robinson swings in 1966 during his first season with Baltimore. That year, Robinson won the AL Triple Crown.

Robinson spent 1966 proving DeWitt wrong. He not only brought his talent to Baltimore, but also a fiery competitive nature that spread across the whole team.

Jim Palmer, a 20-year-old pitcher on the 1966 Orioles, said, "He made everyone believe they could win. You talk about teams that hope to win. That was the Orioles before Frank.

After he got there, we expected to win."

Robinson turned in one of the major leagues' best seasons ever. He won the rare Triple Crown. He led the AL in batting average (.316), home runs (49), and RBIs (122). Robinson also made history by being named the AL's MVP in 1966. He had also been MVP of the NL in 1961 with Cincinnati, making him the first player to be named MVP in both leagues.

Robinson was not the only powerful hitter in the Orioles' lineup that year. Third baseman Brooks Robinson hit 23 homers and drove in 100 runs. First baseman Boog Powell hit 34 home runs with 109 RBIs. The team also featured terrific fielding. Shortstop Luis Aparicio joined Brooks Robinson to give the Orioles a stellar left side of the infield. In center field, Paul Blair was fast enough to track down many balls that seemed headed for base hits. However, the Orioles probably would not have gone 97–63 and won the AL pennant in 1966 if not for their bullpen, with players such as Stu Miller, Moe Drabowsky, and Eddie Watt. Three of Baltimore's starting pitchers experienced injuries, so relief pitchers had to step in to take their places.

"The bullpen was the key to the season," Frank Robinson said. "Those guys were experienced and knew what to do. They didn't ever walk anyone. You had to earn your way on."

Partly because of the Orioles' injuries among their starting pitchers, they were considered big underdogs to the Los Angeles Dodgers in the 1966 World Series. The Orioles were playing in their first World Series. The Dodgers were considered among baseball's elite teams. Los Angeles had terrific pitching, led by arguably the major leagues' best pitcher, Sandy Koufax. As the World Series was about to start, the Orioles saw a billboard in Los Angeles that showed how confident most people felt about the outcome of the best-of-seven Series. It read: "How About Four Straight?"

As it turned out, it was the Orioles who won four straight. They surprised the baseball world. Baltimore's pitchers shut down Los Angeles' batters. The Orioles won Game 1 because Drabowsky pitched 6 2/3 shutout innings in relief. In Game 2, the Orioles beat Koufax on errors by Willie Davis, the Dodgers' usually

Saving the Star

Frank Robinson nearly did not make it through the 1966 season. In late August, with the Orioles comfortably in first place, a friend of the team hosted a party for the players at his home, which had a swimming pool. With everybody having a good time, his teammates insisted Robinson get in the pool. They did not believe it when he said he could not swim, so they pushed him in. People thought he was kidding as he splashed around crying "Help!" and then sank to the bottom of the pool. Catcher Andy Etchebarren eventually dived in to check on Robinson and found it was no joke. Etchebarren pulled Robinson from the pool, saving him from drowning.

Left to right, third baseman Brooks Robinson, catcher Andy Etchebarren, and pitcher Dave McNally celebrate the Orioles' 1966 World Series title.

reliable center fielder. In Baltimore, the Orioles completed the sweep with complete games by pitchers Wally Bunker and Dave McNally.

After Game 4, the headline in the *Baltimore Sun* newspaper read: "Would You Believe Four Straight?"

CHAPTER 4

SEASONS OF GLORY

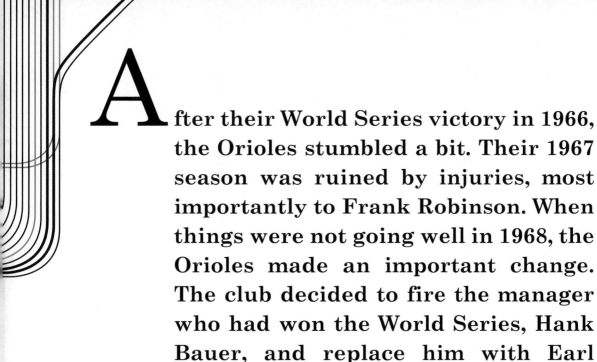

A fter their World Series victory in 1966, the Orioles stumbled a bit. Their 1967 season was ruined by injuries, most importantly to Frank Robinson. When things were not going well in 1968, the Orioles made an important change. The club decided to fire the manager who had won the World Series, Hank Bauer, and replace him with Earl Weaver.

Weaver had been a manager of Orioles minor league teams for years. He was promoted to first-base coach with Baltimore in 1968. He then received another promotion, to manager. Once he was in place, the Orioles started a run of success. From 1968 to 1982, they won six AL East Division titles, four AL championships, and a World Series crown. The Orioles never had a losing season during that time. Weaver stepped down after the 1982 season. The next year,

Manager Earl Weaver argues with home-plate umpire Marty Springstead in July 1974. The feisty Weaver led the Orioles to four AL crowns.

Third baseman Brooks Robinson makes a diving catch during Game 3 of the 1970 World Series. Robinson's defense helped Baltimore win the Series in five games over Cincinnati.

the Orioles won another World Series.

Weaver was not a big man. But he was very scrappy. He had never made it to the major leagues as a player. But he was known for being competitive.

In 1969, the AL and the NL reorganized into leagues with two divisions each and began playing a championship series round of playoffs before the World Series. The winners of the divisions would meet in the championship series (the ALCS and the NLCS), with the winners of those series advancing to the World Series.

The Orioles won the ALCS its first three years, from 1969 to 1971. They also won more than 100 games each season.

Baltimore would stay close in many games because its strong pitching and defense would not allow the other team to score a lot of runs. Then one of the Orioles' power hitters—Frank Robinson, Brooks Robinson, or Boog Powell—might hit a home run.

Baltimore was upset four games to one by the New York Mets in the 1969 World Series. It was just as big a surprise as when the Orioles beat the Los Angeles Dodgers for baseball's championship in 1966.

However, when the Orioles returned to the World Series in 1970, they captured the team's second title. They won four games to one over the Cincinnati Reds. The Orioles' pitchers were able to keep the powerful Reds mostly under control. They got a big hand from Brooks Robinson. He made a number of outstanding plays in the field.

The Reds' Lee May, who lost an apparent base hit to one of Robinson's amazing plays, compared him to a brand of vacuum cleaner. "Where do they plug Mr. Hoover in?" May asked.

The Orioles returned to the World Series in 1971. This time, they lost to the Pittsburgh Pirates in seven games. In 1973 and 1974, Baltimore won the AL East but could not get past the Oakland Athletics in the ALCS.

The Orioles continued to win. But the team was changing. Frank Robinson was traded to the Dodgers after the 1971 season. Powell was dealt to the Cleveland Indians after 1974. Brooks Robinson retired in 1977. In 1976, the Orioles made a big trade with the New York Yankees and received important pieces of their team in that deal—catcher Rick Dempsey and pitchers Scott McGregor and Tippy Martinez.

Baltimore made it to the World Series again in 1979, in a rematch against Pittsburgh. The Orioles led three games to one in the Series. But the Pirates took three games in a row, the final two in Baltimore, to win the world championship.

By 1979, one of the Orioles' next great players, first baseman Eddie Murray, was in place. He was a rarity: a switch-hitter who could hit for power from both sides of the plate. When he retired after 21 seasons, 12 1/2 of them with the Orioles, Murray had driven in more runs than any other switch-hitter in baseball history. The Milwaukee Brewers beat the host Orioles 10–2 in the final game of the 1982 season to edge out Baltimore for the AL East title. Weaver retired after that season.

The Orioles did not miss the postseason the next year under new manager Joe Altobelli, who had been a coach with the Yankees. Led by Murray and shortstop Cal Ripken Jr., who was in his second year, the Orioles won the AL East. They then defeated the Chicago White Sox in the ALCS and beat the Philadelphia Phillies for the World Series title. Murray hit two homers in Game 5 as Baltimore won 5–0 at Philadelphia

Catcher Rick Dempsey (24) hugs pitcher Scott McGregor after the Orioles beat the host Phillies 5–0 in Game 5 to earn the 1983 World Series crown.

to clinch the championship. Dempsey, named MVP of the Series, also homered. McGregor pitched a shutout.

They could not have known it then, but as of 2010, that was the last time the Orioles would make it to the World Series.

CHAPTER **5**

THE MAGIC IS GONE

The Orioles recorded another winning season in 1984, though they were never in contention behind the Detroit Tigers. The Tigers got off to a hot start and ran away with the AL East title. The Orioles also were above .500 in 1985, but again they did not contend for first place.

The team was changing. Pitcher Jim Palmer, the Orioles' all-time leader in wins, strikeouts, and several other categories, saw his career end in 1984. Designated hitter Ken Singleton and outfielder Al Bumbry—key members of the lineup that won the 1983 World Series—were gone after the 1984 season.

Ownership Changes

After Edward Bennett Williams, who had owned the team since 1979, died in 1988, the Orioles were sold to a New York businessman named Eli Jacobs. However, Jacobs ran into financial problems. The team was sold in an auction in court in 1993. The sale price of the team ended up being $173 million. The winning bid was from a group headed by Baltimore lawyer Peter Angelos.

Orioles shortstop Cal Ripken Jr. steps over the Yankees' Rickey Henderson, who steals second base in September 1986. Baltimore finished 73–89 that year for its first losing season since 1967.

Manager Cal Ripken Sr. argues a call on April 9, 1988. Ripken was fired after the team started 0–6 that year. The Orioles would lose their first 21 games, setting a big-league record.

It used to be that the Orioles would mostly replace players by plugging in young talent from the farm system. Though several players from the minor leagues had become Orioles regulars by 1984 and 1985, the team had started to look to free agents as a way to improve the roster. This meant signing players who had established themselves with other teams. The hope was their previous success would continue with the Orioles.

However, that did not work out. Joe Altobelli, the manager when Baltimore won the world championship in 1983, was fired in 1985. Earl Weaver came out of retirement to manage the team again. But he could not turn the Orioles into contenders. The run of winning seasons ended in 1986, and Weaver was done for good this time. In 1987, Cal Ripken Sr., father of All-Star shortstop Cal Ripken Jr., took over as manager. But the losing continued. The Orioles finished 67–95 for their worst season since 1955.

Then came 1988.

The Orioles lost their first 21 games, setting a major league record for most defeats to start a season. After only six games, they fired Ripken Sr. His replacement as manager was former Orioles great Frank Robinson. Baltimore went on to win only 54 games and lose 107. The winning percentage of .335 was even worse than that of the first Orioles team made up of old St. Louis Browns in 1954.

After the season, the Orioles traded All-Star first baseman Eddie Murray to the Los Angeles Dodgers. Once a favorite Oriole, Murray had become the target of criticism as the team declined.

Instead of another losing campaign in 1989, though, the Orioles turned in perhaps their most surprising season. Behind a rallying cry of "Why Not?" the team contended for the AL East title all season. Baltimore fell only two games short of first place. The Orioles still had a chance to win until they lost to the Toronto Blue Jays on the next-to-last day of the season. The Blue Jays won the East.

Unfortunately for the Orioles, 1989 did not launch them into a new winning era. They were back to losing records in 1990 and 1991. At the end of the 1991 season, the Orioles said goodbye to Memorial Stadium. They would move into their new ballpark, Oriole Park at Camden Yards, in 1992. The Orioles' last game at Memorial Stadium, their home since 1954, drew more than 50,000 fans on October 6, 1991.

The team did start to play better after moving into Camden Yards, though the Orioles

1993 All-Star Game

On July 13, 1993, Baltimore was the site of the All-Star Game. The city had hosted the game one time before, in 1958 at Memorial Stadium. The 1993 game was held at the one-year-old Oriole Park at Camden Yards. Before the event, there was a weeklong FanFest held at the Baltimore Convention Center, where fans could enjoy baseball displays and activities. For Orioles fans, the game, won 9–3 by the AL over the NL, might have been most notable for what did not happen. Baltimore's best pitcher, Mike Mussina, started to warm up in the bullpen, but AL manager Cito Gaston of the Toronto Blue Jays did not put Mussina in the game. Orioles fans responded by booing Gaston.

A crowd of 44,568 packs into Oriole Park at Camden Yards on April 6, 1992. The Orioles opened the ballpark with a 2–0 win over the Indians.

did not get close to the playoffs. However, Oriole Park was a big hit with fans. They filled the stadium with sellout crowds night after night. The Orioles drew more than 3.5 million fans to the new stadium, 1 million more than their best season at Memorial Stadium. Even outside Baltimore, people talked about how wonderful Oriole Park was. It was hailed for the way it combined the look of an old ballpark with the touches of the most modern stadiums.

CHAPTER 6

BRIEF COMEBACK

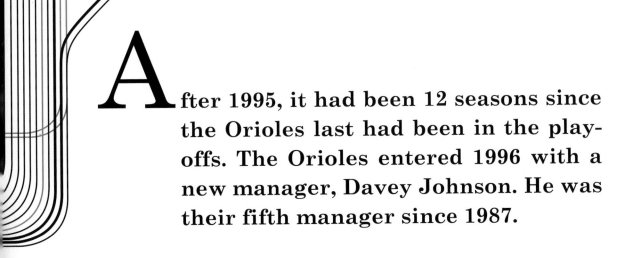

A

fter 1995, it had been 12 seasons since the Orioles last had been in the play-offs. The Orioles entered 1996 with a new manager, Davey Johnson. He was their fifth manager since 1987.

Johnson had been an All-Star second baseman for the Orioles. He had played on their great teams from 1966 to 1972. As manager of the New York Mets and the Cincinnati Reds, Johnson had won four division titles and one World Series.

Under Johnson, the Orioles made the playoffs in 1996 as a wild-card team and then won the AL East in 1997. Both times, the Orioles won the AL Division Series (ALDS) and reached the ALCS but could not win to make the World Series. The division series were extra playoff rounds that were added when the AL and the NL went to three divisions each in 1994.

The Orioles' lineup in 1996 and 1997 was filled with power. In fact, in 1996, Baltimore broke the big-league record for homers in a season, previously held by the 1961 New York Yankees, by

Baltimore's Brady Anderson watches his home run during Game 2 of the 1996 ALDS against Cleveland. The Orioles won 7–4 and would prevail in the series in four games.

hitting 257. The power parade was led by center fielder Brady Anderson, first baseman Rafael Palmeiro, right fielder Bobby Bonilla, and shortstop Cal Ripken Jr. Each of them hit at least 26 homers (led by Anderson's 50) and drove in at least 102 runs (led by Palmeiro's 142). Baltimore also welcomed back Eddie Murray after acquiring him from the Cleveland Indians during the season.

In the ALCS against the Yankees, a home run that should not have been a home run turned out to be the most famous play. In Game 1 in New York, with the Yankees trailing the Orioles by one run in the eighth, New York's Derek Jeter hit a long fly ball to the wall in right field. Orioles outfielder Tony Tarasco was camped under the ball and looked ready to catch it. But a 12-year-old Yankees fan named Jeffrey Maier reached out over the fence and knocked the ball into the stands. The umpire ruled it was a home run. The Yankees tied the score, then won in extra innings. They went on to win the series in five games.

In 1997, the Orioles went 98–64 and won the AL East. The biggest change was with Ripken. The Orioles acquired a new shortstop, Mike Bordick, and moved Ripken to third base. In the ALCS against Cleveland, Orioles ace Mike Mussina pitched two great games. But the Orioles lost both times in extra innings. The Indians won the series in six games.

After 1997, Orioles fans had a lot less to cheer about.

Orioles right fielder Tony Tarasco stretches for the ball as Yankees fan Jeffrey Maier, *top middle*, knocks it into the stands in Game 1 of the 1996 ALCS. The play was ruled a home run for New York's Derek Jeter.

CHAPTER 7

WAITING TO WIN AGAIN

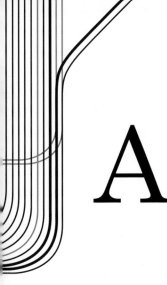

After 1997, the Orioles went into a long down period. Through 2010, they had not had a single winning season.

Davey Johnson, who had led the team to two straight playoff berths, left after 1997. On the day he was named AL Manager of the Year, Johnson resigned. Johnson and owner Peter Angelos did not get along. When Johnson asked for a contract extension, Angelos said no. So Johnson quit.

Ray Miller, who had been the Orioles' pitching coach when they had some of the major leagues' best pitching, took over as manager. Miller would turn out to be one of seven managers the Orioles had from 1998 to 2010. During that time, the closest the Orioles came to a winning record was in 1998. They finished 79–83 that year.

The farm system, which once had restocked the Orioles with players, no longer

Slugger Albert Belle, shown in 1999, put up impressive statistics in two years with the Orioles, but his behavior was sometimes poor. Beginning in 1998, Baltimore went on a long run of losing seasons.

was producing. After 2001, the team's biggest star, Cal Ripken Jr., retired. The regular lineup for 2002 included only one player, second baseman Jerry Hairston, who had been drafted and come up through the minors with the Orioles. Many of the players who rose to the majors were not of big-league quality.

In October 2007, the man in charge of the Orioles' farm system, David Stockstill, said, "We're still bringing up players from Double-A and Triple-A who are not really ready to go to the big leagues, step on the field, and help a championship club."

As the team continued to post losing seasons, the attendance at Oriole Park went down. In 2008, the total attendance at Camden Yards fell to less than 2 million for the first time since the Orioles moved

Waste of Money

The Orioles once were a model of efficiency in the management of the team. But a sign of how far things had fallen happened in 1999. The Orioles signed pitcher Xavier Hernandez to a two-year, $2.5 million contract and announced the deal. However, they had not given Hernandez a medical exam yet. When they did, the Orioles found out Hernandez had an injured shoulder. Owner Peter Angelos decided he did not want to add an injured pitcher to the team. Because the deal had been announced, though, the Orioles still ended up having to pay Hernandez most of the money, even though he never pitched for them.

into the ballpark in 1992. When the New York Yankees or the Boston Red Sox came to town, their fans would fill Camden Yards. Cheers for those teams could make it sound as if the games were being played in New York or Boston.

Though a lot of free agents did not want to sign with the

Cal Ripken Jr. raises his cap to the Boston crowd as former Red Sox star Dwight Evans stands with him on September 27, 2001. Ripken, who was retiring at the end of that season, was honored with a farewell ceremony.

Orioles because of their poor records, the team made a big signing for the 1999 season. Baltimore brought in Albert Belle, one of the major leagues' top hitters. In 1998, Belle batted .328 with 49 home runs and 152 RBIs for the Chicago White Sox. The Orioles gave Belle a five-year, $65 million contract.

Belle had behaved badly in his career, clashing with fans and the press. The same behavior resurfaced in Baltimore.

During one 1999 game at Oriole Park, Belle made a crude gesture to fans who were heckling him. Belle ended up posting productive statistics as a hitter. He drove in more than 100 runs in 1999 and 2000. But he had a hip injury that would not get better. He could not play after 2000. The Orioles ended up being stuck with paying most of his big salary for three years when Belle did not play.

As the losing seasons continued, individual Orioles still posted notable performances. Shortstop Miguel Tejada drove in 150 runs in 2004. In 2009, All-Star second baseman Brian Roberts set a major league record for most doubles by a switch-hitter with 56. Roberts also became just the fourth big-league player to have three seasons with at least 50 doubles.

In 2006, right fielder Nick Markakis emerged with a standout rookie season for Baltimore. He batted .291 with 16 homers and 62 RBIs. Markakis improved from there, hitting .300 with 23 homers and 112 RBIs in 2007 and continuing his strong play during the next several seasons.

More good news arrived for the Orioles in May 2009. That

Palmeiro Controversy

In 2005, the Orioles found themselves in the middle of baseball's steroids controversy. Steroids are a kind of drug that can help a player get stronger, but they are illegal and dangerous to one's health. Baltimore first baseman Rafael Palmeiro tested positive for a performance-enhancing drug. Major League Baseball suspended him in August. Palmeiro was one of baseball's consistently outstanding hitters. Earlier that season, he had collected the 3,000th hit of his career. Even worse was that in March 2005, Palmeiro had testified in Congress about steroids. He had waved his finger and said he never used steroids.

Second baseman Brian Roberts, shown in 2009, was a consistent bright spot for the Orioles even though the team continued to struggle.

month, promising catcher Matt Wieters was called up from the minor leagues and made his debut with Baltimore. Wieters had a strong rookie campaign, batting .288 with nine homers and 43 RBIs.

By 2010, the powerful Yankees and Red Sox had been joined as playoff contenders by the Tampa Bay Rays in the AL East. The Orioles still seemed a long way from returning to the playoffs. But with Markakis and Wieters leading the way and other prospects gaining big-league experience, Baltimore had hope that it could turn things around.

TIMELINE

1953 AL owners approve the sale of the St. Louis Browns to an ownership group from Baltimore.

1954 The Baltimore Orioles play their first season. They win their first game at Memorial Stadium, 3–1 over the Chicago White Sox on April 15, but finish the season 54–100.

1965 After the season, the Orioles trade with the Cincinnati Reds for All-Star outfielder Frank Robinson.

1966 With Robinson, the AL MVP, leading the way, the Orioles finish 97–63, win the pennant, and then beat the favored Los Angeles Dodgers four games to none in the World Series.

1969 The Orioles finish a team-best 109–53 and win the AL pennant but are upset four games to one in the World Series by the New York Mets.

1970 Baltimore goes 108–54. The Orioles return to the World Series and win it this time. They beat the Cincinnati Reds four games to one.

1971 The Orioles finish 101–57 and make it to another World Series, in which they lose four games to three to the Pittsburgh Pirates.

1979 In the season in which "Orioles Magic" is born, Baltimore faces Pittsburgh in the World Series for the second time in the 1970s. Though the Orioles lead the Series 3–1 after four games, the Pirates take the title by winning the last three games, including the final two in Baltimore.

1983
Led by first baseman Eddie Murray and shortstop Cal Ripken Jr., the Orioles defeat the White Sox in the ALCS and then beat the Philadelphia Phillies four games to one in the World Series.

1988
The Orioles set a major league record by losing their first 21 games of the season.

1992
Oriole Park at Camden Yards opens. On April 6, Baltimore defeats the Cleveland Indians 2–0 in the first game at the new stadium.

1995
On September 6, Ripken breaks Lou Gehrig's record for consecutive games by playing in his 2,131st in a row. The Orioles defeat the visiting California Angels 4–2.

1996
The Orioles make the playoffs. In Game 1 of the ALCS at Yankee Stadium on October 9, a 12-year-old fan interferes with a ball that is ruled a home run for the Yankees. The Orioles fall 5–4 and go on to lose the series four games to one.

1997
The Orioles stay in first place in the AL East all season, finishing 98–64. Baltimore beats the Seattle Mariners three games to one in the ALDS but falls four games to two to Cleveland in the ALCS.

1998
Ripken ends his playing streak at 2,632 games, sitting out the Orioles' 5–4 loss to the visiting Yankees on September 20.

2010
The Orioles complete their 13th losing season in a row.

QUICK STATS

FRANCHISE HISTORY

Milwaukee Brewers (1901)
St. Louis Browns (1902–53)
Baltimore Orioles (1954–)

WORLD SERIES
(wins in bold)

1944, **1966**, 1969, **1970**, 1971, 1979, **1983**

AL CHAMPIONSHIP SERIES
(1969–)

1969, 1970, 1971, 1973, 1974, 1979, 1983, 1996, 1997

DIVISION CHAMPIONSHIPS
(1969–)

1969, 1970, 1971, 1973, 1974, 1979, 1983, 1997

KEY PLAYERS
(position[s]; seasons with team)

Paul Blair (OF; 1964–76)
Mike Cuellar (SP; 1969–76)
Dave McNally (SP; 1962–74)
Eddie Murray (1B; 1977–88, 1996)
Mike Mussina (SP; 1991–2000)
Jim Palmer (SP; 1965–67, 1969–84)
Boog Powell (OF/1B; 1961–74)
Cal Ripken Jr. (SS/3B; 1981–2001)
Brian Roberts (2B/SS; 2001–)
Brooks Robinson (3B; 1955–77)
Frank Robinson (OF; 1966–71)
George Sisler (1B; 1915–22, 1924–27)

KEY MANAGERS

Hank Bauer (1964–68):
    407–318; 4–0 (postseason)
Earl Weaver (1968–82, 1985–86):
    1,480–1,060; 26–20 (postseason)

HOME PARKS

Lloyd Street Grounds (1901)
Sportsman's Park (1902–53)
Memorial Stadium (1954–91)
Oriole Park at Camden Yards
    (1992–)

* All statistics through 2010 season

QUOTES AND ANECDOTES

On July 8, 1958, Baltimore hosted the All-Star Game for the first time. Orioles pitcher Billy O'Dell got the last nine NL hitters out to give the AL a 4–3 win.

"All of a sudden, you could see it. Everyone was thinking, 'Now we got it. We got the hitter we needed, and we're going to win.'"
—Dick Hall, Orioles pitcher, on the arrival of Frank Robinson before the 1966 season

One of the things that made the Orioles consistent winners in the Earl Weaver era was their pitching. From 1968 through 1980, they had at least one pitcher who won 20 games every year. In 1971, they became just the second team in major league history to have four 20-game winners in one season. They were Mike Cuellar (20–9), Pat Dobson (20–8), Dave McNally (21–5), and Jim Palmer (20–9).

Before the Orioles' Cal Ripken Jr. came along in the early 1980s, players who were much taller than six feet were considered too tall to play shortstop. The position used to be reserved for smaller players because baseball people thought bigger men could not make the quick fielding plays of a shortstop. But Ripken is 6-foot-4, and he was an outstanding fielder. He won two Gold Gloves, given to the best fielder at each position. After Ripken, several taller shortstops became stars in the majors, such as Derek Jeter, Alex Rodriguez, and Troy Tulowitzki, all of whom are 6-foot-3.

GLOSSARY

acquire

To add a player, usually through the draft, free agency, or a trade.

auction

Where something is sold to whoever bids the most money.

berth

A place, spot, or position, such as in the baseball playoffs.

contender

A team that is in the race for a championship or playoff berth.

designated hitter

A position used only in the American League. Managers can employ an extra hitter in the batting order who comes to the plate to hit instead of the pitcher.

farm system

A big-league club's teams in the minor leagues, where players are developed for the majors.

franchise

An entire sports organization, including the players, coaches, and staff.

pennant

A flag. In baseball, it symbolizes that a team has won its league championship.

postseason

The games in which the best teams play after the regular-season schedule has been completed.

retire

To officially end one's career.

rookie

A first-year player in the major leagues.

roster

The players as a whole on a baseball team.

scrappy

Always ready to fight.

FOR MORE INFORMATION

Further Reading

Berney, Louis. *Tales from the Orioles Dugout*. Champaign, IL: Sports Publishing, 2004.

Gesker, Michael, and Brooks Robinson. *The Orioles Encyclopedia: A Half Century of History and Highlights*. Baltimore: The Johns Hopkins University Press, 2009.

Ripken, Cal, Jr. *My Story*. New York: Dial Books, 1999.

Web Links

To learn more about the Baltimore Orioles, visit ABDO Publishing Company online at **www.abdopublishing.com**. Web sites about the Orioles are featured on our Book Links page. These links are routinely monitored and updated to provide the most current information available.

Places to Visit

National Baseball Hall of Fame and Museum
25 Main Street
Cooperstown, NY 13326
1-888-HALL-OF-FAME
www.baseballhall.org
This hall of fame and museum highlights the greatest players and moments in the history of baseball. Cal Ripken Jr. is among the former Orioles enshrined here.

Oriole Park at Camden Yards
333 West Camden Street
Baltimore, MD 21201
410-685-9800
http://mlb.mlb.com/bal/ballpark/index.jsp
This has been the Orioles' home field since 1992.

Sports Legends Museum at Camden Yards
301 West Camden Street
Baltimore, MD 21201
410-727-1539
www.baberuthmuseum.com
This museum is located next door to Oriole Park and near the Babe Ruth Birthplace Museum, which operates the Sports Legends Museum. A lot of the museum is dedicated to the Orioles, including uniforms used by the players.

INDEX

About the Author

Ray Frager is a freelance writer based in the Baltimore, Maryland, area. He has been a professional sports editor and writer since 1980. He has worked for the *Trenton Times*, the *Dallas Morning News*, the *Baltimore Sun*, and FOXSports.com. At the *Sun*, he edited books on Cal Ripken Jr., the building of Baltimore's football stadium, and the Baltimore Ravens' 2000 Super Bowl season.